Charlie & Wilbur's SPOOKY MAZES

Written and illustrated by

Patrick Merrell

Sterling Publishing Co., Inc.
New York

Dedicated to:

Peter,
Frances,
& Meredith

2 4 6 8 10 9 7 5 3 1

Published by Sterling Publishing Co., Inc.
387 Park Avenue South, New York, NY 10016
© 2007 by Patrick Merrell
Book design by Patrick Merrell
Distributed in Canada by Sterling Publishing
c/o Canadian Manda Group, 165 Dufferin Street,
Toronto, Ontario, Canada M6K 3H6
Distributed in the United Kingdom by GMC Distribution Services,
Castle Place, 166 High Street, Lewes, East Sussex, England BN7 1XU
Distributed in Australia by Capricorn Link (Australia) Pty. Ltd.
P.O. Box 704, Windsor, NSW 2756, Australia

Printed in China

Sterling ISBN-13: 978-1-4027-3801-2
ISBN-10: 1-4027-3801-3

For information about custom editions, special sales, premium and
corporate purchases, please contact Sterling Special Sales
Department at 800-805-5489 or specialsales@sterlingpub.com.

Charlie, a crocodile, and Wilbur, a turtle, were best friends.

They lived a very long time ago—back when dinosaurs roamed the earth.

Mazes were their favorite thing in the whole world—finding them, making them and, most of all, solving them!

It was the day of the big SPOOKFEST party, and Charlie and Wilbur still hadn't decided on their costumes.

"I really want to win the best costume prize this year," Wilbur said.

"Me, too," said Charlie. "Maybe my new issue of DINO DIGEST will give us an idea." It was a special SPOOKFEST issue.

Charlie turned to the maze section in the back first. "Ooh! One of my favorites—a MUTTABURRASAURUS!" Charlie said.

"He looks a bit scared," Wilbur said.

"Wouldn't *you* be scared with all those ghosts around?" Charlie said.

This Muttaburrasaurus needs to get to SAFETY.
Find the one route that doesn't lead to a ghost.

"Yikes! Duck!" Charlie yelped when Wilbur turned the page.
"Those aren't ducks," Wilbur said. "They're QUETZALCOATLUS."
"Good one, Wilbur," Charlie chuckled.

DINO FACT: QUETZALCOATLUS, a flying reptile, was probably the largest flying creature ever. Its wingspan could reach nearly 15 feet—as long as a car!

The last maze was an OVIRAPTOR.

"I wouldn't want to run into that fella in a dark alley," Wilbur said, shuddering.

"I wouldn't want to run into him in a *bright* alley!" Charlie added.

They both chuckled.

"Well, that was fun," Wilbur said, "but what about our costumes?!"
Charlie found the answer when he turned the page of his magazine.
"Hey, look at this!" he said. "There's a sale at Chumley's House of
Costumes!" The ad included a map.

Note: There are many one-way streets in this maze. You can move only in the direction the arrows are pointing.

"What are we waiting for?!" Wilbur said.
"Chumley's, here we come!" Charlie added.
The backyard was dotted with shadows from the clouds above.
"No stepping on the dark parts!" Charlie said.
"Heh heh, this is fun," Wilbur said.

When they got around to the front yard, Charlie remembered that his bike had a broken chain.

"We're going to have to take the bus," Charlie said. Unfortunately, the quickest way to the bus stop was through Dead Tree Swamp.

Dead Tree Swamp

Start

"But there are creepy, crawly things in there!" Wilbur said. "Probably things left over from the PRECAMBRIAN ERA!" He shuddered at the thought.

"Don't worry," Charlie said. "I'll scare 'em off for you."

This made Wilbur smile a bit...but not much.

DINO FACT:
The PRECAMBRIAN ERA, about 5 billion years long, was a period of time before crocodiles, turtles, and dinosaurs lived.

They got to the bus stop with a few minutes to spare.

A map of the bus route was posted on a pole next to the bench.

"Hmm," Wilbur said. "I see a route that goes to every stop just once without going over the same path twice."

"Ooh, ooh! Let me see if I can find it!" Charlie said.

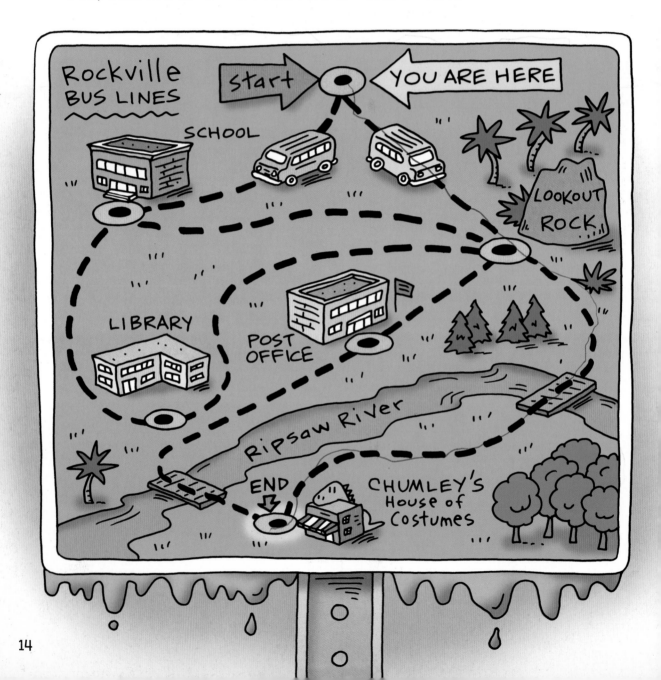

When the bus arrived, Charlie and Wilbur went all the way to the backseat, their favorite spot.

"Hey, look," Charlie said. "The spiderweb in this broken window is a maze."

"Woo hoo!" Wilbur said. "Let's solve it!"

It was a long bus ride. To help pass the time, Wilbur decided to draw a maze in his sketchbook.

He ended up drawing two mazes!

"My turn! My turn!" Charlie said.
"Sure thing," Wilbur said as he handed him his sketchbook.
Charlie's maze filled two pages.

DINO FACT: *STAURIKOSAURUS was one of the very first dinosaurs to appear on earth, about 230 million years ago.*

Unfortunately, that wasn't the end of their troubles. As they drove over a badly cracked section of road, a loud bang came from the back of the bus.

When they got out, they saw that the bus had a flat tire.

Pfft

"Sorry, folks, this bus isn't going anywhere," the driver said. "We don't have a spare tire." A loud moan came from the passengers.

"But not to worry," he said. "The train station is nearby—right across the cemetery." The moan from the passengers was even louder this time.

At the train station, Charlie and Wilbur studied the routes to figure out which train to take.

"That station at CYCAD Street is right next to Chumley's," Wilbur said.

"But the train that goes there won't arrive for another hour!" Charlie said. They weren't sure what to do.

Note: Follow the train tracks only as a train would. No going backward or making left or right turns where the tracks cross.

DINO FACT: *CYCAD trees are ancient evergreens that look a lot like palm trees. They still grow today in many warm parts of the world!*

Luckily, a SILVISAURUS overheard Charlie and Wilbur and had the perfect solution.

"I know two DIMORPHODONS that will fly you anywhere you want to go," she said. "They live just on the other side of Thorn Park." She pointed across the street to a park filled with prickly thorn trees.

25

Drake and Grizelda, an old DIMORPHODON couple, were more than happy to fly Charlie and Wilbur to Chumley's.

But Wilbur wasn't so sure. "It'll cost us half of the money we were going to use for our costumes," he whispered. "And just look at them—they might eat us!"

"Don't worry," Charlie said. "We'll have enough money left—and most of their teeth have fallen out anyway!"

Note: Follow the flying routes to find out which one Drake and Grizelda took.

As it turned out, Wilbur had little reason to worry. Drake and Grizelda were a bit creepy looking, but they were harmless.

"Thanks!" Charlie and Wilbur said as they hopped off and darted across the street. They had to weave their way through the tail end of the town's annual SPOOKFEST parade.

Note: Follow the paths from "Start" to discover where they lead.

Chumley's was very cluttered inside. Charlie and Wilbur quickly made their way to the back counter.

"Hurry," Wilbur said. "There's not much time left before the party starts!"

Start

End
Back Counter

to storage and changing rooms

There was a large price chart, and it took some doing to figure out how much each costume cost. They finally discovered the only costumes they could afford were the two that were on sale.

"We'll take one of each!" Charlie said, plunking nearly all of their money down on the counter.

Note: Follow the lines to find out which two costumes they could afford.

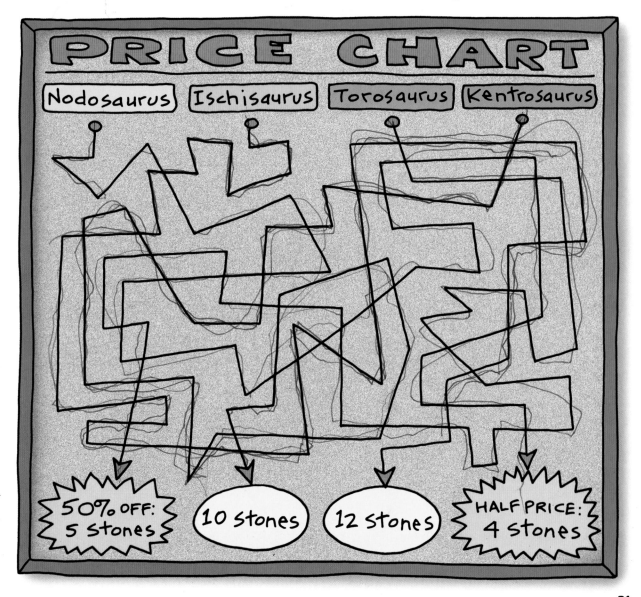

"These NODOSAURUS and TOROSAURUS costumes are perfect," Wilbur said as they scurried to the changing rooms. "We'll be the hit of the party!"

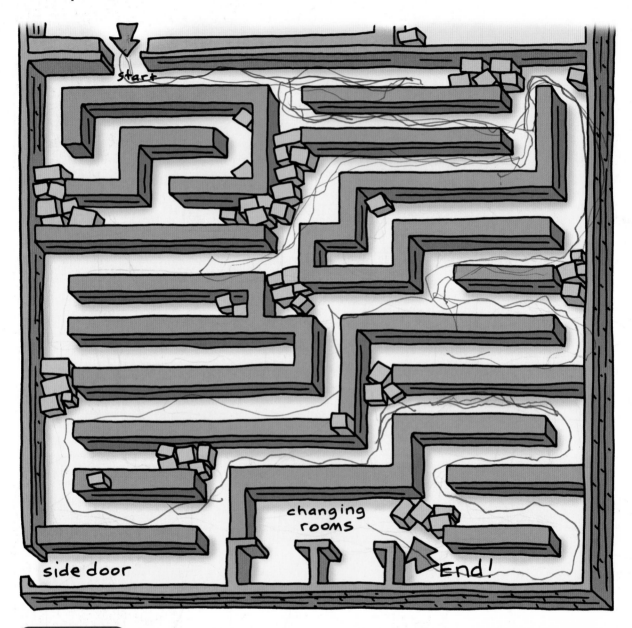

DINO FACT: *The skull of the TOROSAURUS, which was perhaps the largest ever of any land animal, could be more than 8 feet long—the length of a horse!*

To avoid going back through the cluttered store, they scampered out the side door. Unfortunately, the alley was just as big a mess!
"Follow me," Charlie said. "I think I can see the street."

When they got to the sidewalk, they quickly flagged down a taxi. A cab driven by a SHANTUNGOSAURUS pulled over almost immediately.

"To the SPOOKFEST party on the double!" Charlie barked to the driver. The driver hit the gas, and the cab sped into the Haunted Forest, where the party was being held.

Start

When they got to the mansion, Charlie quickly paid the driver.
"It looks like everybody's already inside," Wilbur said.
"Perfect!" Charlie said. "It'll make our entrance all the more dramatic."
As they raced through a tangled trail of ropes leading to the front
doors, they smiled at the thought of everyone admiring their fine outfits.

When they got to the end, they pulled open the large front doors, and then called out, "TA-DAH! HERE WE ARE!"

Charlie's and Wilbur's jaws dropped in amazement. Everyone was dressed exactly like they were! Filling the ballroom was a sea of NODOSAURS and TOROSAURS.

"Hmm," Wilbur said. "I think Chumley's has been busy."

"I guess it's a tie, then," Charlie said. "*Everyone* wins best costume!"

They both chuckled, and then joined the party.

THE ANSWERS

PAGE 5

PAGES 6-7

PAGE 8

PAGE 9

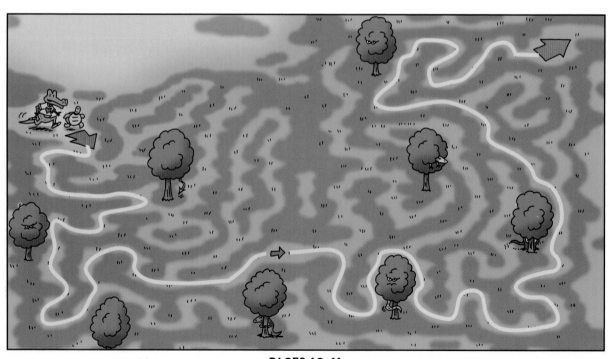

PAGES 10-11

PAGES 12-13

PAGE 14

PAGE 15

PAGE 16

PAGE 17

PAGES 18-19

PAGES 20-21

PAGE 22

PAGE 23

PAGE 24

PAGE 25

PAGES 26-27

PAGES 28-29

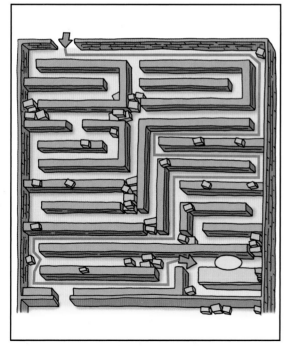

PAGE 30

PAGE 31

PAGE 32

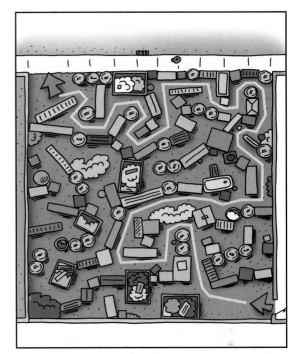

PAGE 33

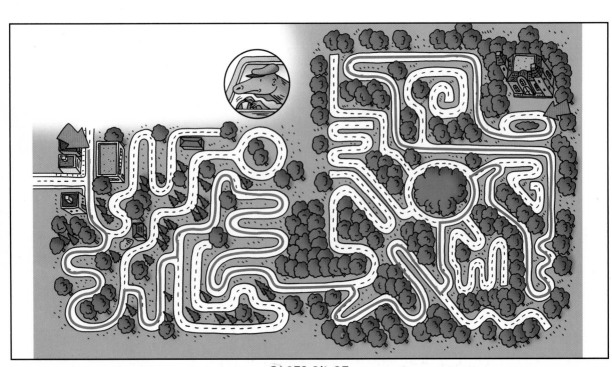

PAGES 34-35

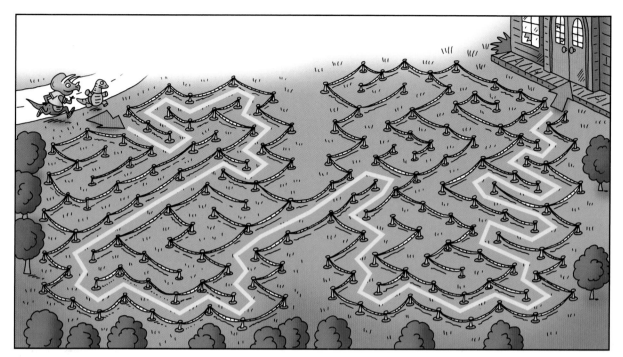

PAGES 36-37

"SPOOKY" DINO FACTS

LARGEST MEAT EATER ▶

GIGANOTOSAURUS might win that title. It weighed 80 tons, about the same as 23 hippos, and had teeth as long as carving knives.

◀ MOST TEETH

Bad news: HADROSAURUS might have had as many as 900 teeth. Good news: HADROSAURUS was a plant eater.

BIGGEST CLAWS ▶

THERIZINOSAURUS is certainly a contender. Each of its fingers had a giant hook-like claw over 2 feet long!

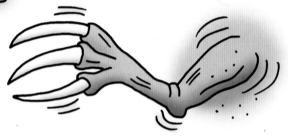

◀ THICKEST SKULL

PACHYCEPHALOSAURUS had an 8-inch-thick dome of bone on its head that it might have used to head-butt other dinosaurs.

WATCH OUT! ▶

STEGOSAURUS had 4 sharp spikes (called a thagomizer) at the end of its powerful, flexible tail.